PROJECT RISE UP

A Self-Care Guide Towards Optimal
Wellness and Performance

KULWINDER SURI

Project Rise Up
Copyright © 2022 by Kulwinder Suri

Tellwell Talent
www.tellwell.ca

ISBN
978-0-2288-7386-0 (Hardcover)
978-0-2288-7385-3 (Paperback)

Table of Contents

I wouldn't be here if it wasn't
for the grace of God.

Thank you for blessing me,
teaching me and guiding me
through this journey of life.

Waheguru

To all those who continue to work on
themselves from the mind, body and soul,

I dedicate this book to you.
Keep on keeping on.

Love and light

INTRODUCTION

What is mental health? Why is there increased awareness around this topic? And what can we do to improve our physical, emotional and spiritual state of well-being?

These are all important questions that have become essential in understanding and applying to our day-to-day lives, and although they may seem common, or easy to grasp for some, most can find matters concerning mental health difficult to comprehend and practice in their lives.

In my own journey, like many others', I've dealt with anxiety, fear, depression, loss and self-doubt that accumulated into a cycle of continuous roadblocks. It wasn't until I reached rock bottom that I decided to sit back and observe my thoughts and emotions. The suffering and pain became so unbearable that a day without a negative mindset seemed foreign and unpleasant. My path to recovery soon began after experiencing terrible anxiety that left me feeling sick to my stomach. The bodily symptoms, along with feeling numb and exhausted, were accompanied by a sense of hopelessness when my personal life was experiencing rejection from my career.

I knew that I needed to break the night with colour and discover myself in a deeper, more profound way.

I began to focus my attention towards positive outlets, whether those be prayers, motivational podcasts or anything to do with hope and inspiration. So many discoveries about the world of mental health were right in front of my eyes. I realized I was in the eye of the storm and that my purpose here on earth was beginning to unfold. I was here to face my fears and to conquer them with strength and courage. Faith had allowed me to see my vision clearly, to become a beacon of hope. Discovering the importance of mental health and working within myself to help nourish the soul was allowing me to see a whole new world, one filled with unconditional love and promise. I was beginning to see that there indeed was light at the end of the tunnel and that the roadmap to get there was always in my control. A lesson was being taught that we each have the power to control our own narrative and switch the paradigm.

Mental health can mean different things for different people, but the overall perception is clear: it's a state of well-being. It refers to how someone copes with the stresses life can bring, how productive one can be and whether a person's decisions are creating healthier habits or self-destructing patterns. Ultimately, these choices are in our control, but there are more and more people self-sabotaging with poor choices. We live in a time in which negativity sells. A lot of the mainstream entertainment glorifies the use of drugs, violence and gangs. It has become apparent that there is more nihilism among society and hatred between one another. Many people are also tied in heavily to accepting lives they do not want, despite the detrimental effects on their physical and emotional well-being.

Like others, I've had to put aside the activities and interests that made me feel whole to follow a system that rewarded me with a simple paycheque. When we get overwhelmed with work that doesn't fulfill our desires, not only does it create an unhealthy mindset, but it leaves us feeling anxious. The thought of being in the present moment fades away because, for many of us, we only look forward in anticipation to days off being our saving grace. This feeling of being trapped causes a ripple effect that leads to more destructive behaviours being passed around from one person to another.

Think about this example: someone who is angry, stressed and depleted in their job will not be truly happy when they hear that a co-worker is being promoted or receiving a higher bonus. It's also more likely that the person who is feeling overwhelmed with pressure in their daily lives will not engage in productive activities such as meditation, journaling, physical activities or even consuming healthier foods. This is the reason that the concept of the mind, body and spirit connection is so important. And yet it is undervalued. Now, imagine someone practicing mindfulness, focusing inwardly and doing a job they enjoyed: they would most likely be more healthy, energetic, attentive, helpful and encouraging to their co-workers, peers and loved ones. They have allowed themselves to fill their own cup of contentment before filling others' with the overflowing juices of radiant love and energy.

We know that being in a positive state of well-being allows us to make better choices, thus creating consistent and progressive habits, yet there still seems to be a struggle to evolve and grow.

Throughout my journey, I've spoken to many people and pondered my thoughts during the days when there was nothing but bleak darkness, and the opinion I carried was evidently similar to others in the same situation: it's easier said than done.

We tend to believe that those who are earning an incredible income have won the lottery and have found their dream jobs, and they are the ones who preach this message of positivity, but for the common individual, it's not relatable. I feel the majority of us have accepted this idea without evidence. From personal experience, I can say that I felt this way simply because I chose not to act on accountability, but rather excuses and self-pity. We must understand that reality is a mindset. We must make a positive shift by altering our thoughts and perceptions.

Take me, for example. I've spent the last eight years working in the financial sector. The many roles I've had within my job throughout the years have mostly involved wearing a headset and speaking to clients about their finances. The number of people I have seen who work similar jobs and experience stress and mental breakdowns is far too high to count. The overall toll these jobs have taken on my physical and

mental health is difficult to explain.
I spent years despising my work and
the negative effects it has had on me.
I never enjoyed the work I was doing,
nor was I happy with the income I was
generating. I felt, however, that my
potential was maximized and that I
would be doing this work for the rest
of my life.

As grateful as I was, and am, my
health was deteriorating, my energy
was declining and I was completely
burnt out. It wasn't until early last year
that I decided to request a lightened
schedule, which was granted. I spent

close to four months working a part-time schedule and, although my income had reduced because of the hours, it turned out to be a blessing in disguise. I began to spend time peeling the layers off my thoughts, emotions, habits and beliefs, and I started to really dig deep within myself.

As someone who's also been certified as a health and life coach, one of the most fundamental observations and concepts I've learned is to examine the "why beneath the why." I started to question why I was doing certain things. Why was I thinking the way

I was, making choices out of fear and cultivating destructive habits? It became apparent that I had filled myself with anxiety and a negative mindset from an early age without even knowing it. I didn't believe in myself, which is one of the worst things you can do. I began to notice that it wasn't my job or circumstances that were exhausting me, it was how I perceived those situations.

I've always had a passion for holistic health. I became obsessed with nutrition and overall well-being, and felt that to achieve happiness and success I had to get into a career in that environment. However, although I am a firm believer in following interests, I soon began to recognize that it wasn't the external factors that were limiting my cheerfulness, it was my mindset. I was allowing the noise around me to dictate my health, my choices, my career and my overall well-being. I began to believe that I had no say in my destiny and that the words of others were a glimpse of truth, and this was undoubtedly causing me to sink into more self-doubt and suffering.

The brain is the most powerful tool in the world, but without knowing it we have allowed it to control us. We've allowed ourselves to consume negativity and build more of it, which is why so much around us—from the food we eat to the news we view to the actions we witness—have become toxic, to say the least. As long as we fail to apply self-care in its purest essence, the concept of spiritual awakening, inner happiness and peace on earth will remain a mere fantasy.

As we move forward in this book, I want to clarify something from the start: You are *not* a failure!

We have allowed factors in our surroundings—whether they be the opinions of others, misleading cultural traditions or the false stories we tell ourselves to evaluate our success—to affect us, and we judge our importance based on what we have externally accomplished. For the longest time I felt I was behind or avoiding success because of society's rules and conditions, yet all along I was being born again through the grace of God to discover myself and share my story. Our mindset is what truly commands the outcome and writes the stories we tell ourselves. As you move forward in this book, you'll begin to realize there are several important pillars that are all within our reach and that hold an interconnection to one another. I will highlight those in the following chapters. Take a moment to remind yourself that you are exactly where you need to be. It's now time to rise up and take back our power, end the stigma surrounding mental health, prioritize our well-being and, once and for all, be *above the noise.*

GRATITUDE

I can't begin to explain how the power
of gratitude has changed my life. My
perspective shifted one hundred and
eighty degrees once I started to truly
understand this act of appreciation.
Before I dive in any further, I want
you to understand that I am not sitting
on some remote island at the moment.

I am not surrounded by paradise filled with beautiful scenery, drinking Champagne and eating exotic fruits. I don't have a bank account filled with millions of dollars, I don't drive fancy cars and I don't currently have the job of my dreams. Quite the contrary. The reason I am explaining this is because it exemplifies how the battle I fought to understand the true meaning of gratitude was initially based on a negative mindset. I used to believe that those who addressed and believed in the power of gratitude could only be the ones who lived this lavish lifestyle and had everything they ever wanted right at their fingertips. I felt they didn't experience the same struggle and setbacks that life tends to bring to the average person. I was naive, I was jealous and I was bitter. I was reluctant to change my ways until I felt I could receive those same comforts and luxuries.

When I reached the lowest point in my life, I found myself at a crossroad. Circumstances around me were beginning to signal that I needed to focus within. The road I found myself on was cold, dark, frightening and lonely. I knew that the only way out of this state of misery was to look deep within myself. I had no other choice. Either self-destructive patterns were going to continue and develop, resulting in more unhappiness, or I was finally going to find my way out and into a world filled with hope. It was difficult, to say the least. My body was numb. I didn't understand why these things were happening to me. I witnessed people use politics in their careers to get themselves into higher-paying positions, and here I was facing rejection and being told I wasn't qualified when I felt I was passionate enough to excel and succeed. My mental health was crumbling to pieces. I experienced constant losses, criticism and defeat. I refused to speak to others about the inner battles I was facing. I didn't want sympathy from others. I am a man of faith, and regardless of the pain I was encountering, I believed in God with all my heart.

As cliché as it sounds, that alone eventually became my saving grace. When I reached the lowest of the lows, it was only then I gave myself to the Lord. I asked for forgiveness, I asked for patience and I asked to be found. Little by little, my prayers brought me into light. The first thing I had to accept to move past my trauma was *accountability*. I had to take ownership of why I was experiencing these feelings and finding myself in a series of negative circumstances that never seemed to go away. It's easy to point the finger and play the blame game by accusing others of responsibility for your displeasure. When we operate solely from the state of our ego, it's challenging and often intolerable to admit to our responsibilities. However, when we accept ourselves for who we truly are, both the good and the bad, we are able to adapt and grow. A question to ask yourself is: How can we teach our children, our upcoming generations and ourselves the importance of self-care and inner work when we are so fixated on blaming others and not owning up to our mistakes?

When we learn to accept accountability, we are able to develop a sense of awareness. The moment I realized it was a lack of effort on my end for not achieving the specific goals I had set out for myself, I started to notice my mind shifting inwardly and away from external blaming factors. An awareness developed, and I was able to identify why I was choosing to feel the way I was. Through self-discovery, it became apparent that I had watered thoughts for years that made me believe I was incapable of accomplishing anything. All along I was searching for an answer, a solution, a formula to help me grow into the person I wanted to be, and yet here I was at the age of thirty-five, finally realizing that the cure had always been within me. By letting go of my ego and taking ownership, along with developing a sense of awareness, I earned the tools I needed to create an action plan.

The first weapon of faith was understanding all I was grateful for. Having gratitude is the door that opens to unlimited miracles. We may not have all the things we want, but when we begin to pour love into all that we have, it allows us to feel satiated and contented. There is an illusion that floats around within human nature that having more leads to more happiness. We are always searching outwardly to find something that we believe will give us inner bliss. Whether it's a career change, a higher salary, a brand-new vehicle, the latest pair of shoes or a relationship, there is always this idea that having it will solve all our problems. In all fairness, it is difficult for people to think otherwise. The media around us can fuel this concept and give it the appearance of truth. Whether it's television advertisements or entertainment avenues such as music videos, song lyrics, movies or the overall use of social media, the perception of having more seems to point towards an increased level of happiness and achievement.

Here's a few questions to think about. When was the last time you fell in love with wanting to purchase something?

And when you finally bought it, after a few months, how did you feel about that item? Did it still bring that same joy to you as it did before actually owning it? Chances are that the attraction and excitement you once placed on that item has waned, and it no longer holds the same level of desire.

What we fail to understand is that the behaviour of always wanting more is what keeps us farther away from experiencing gratitude in its wholesomeness. There is nothing wrong with wanting the gift of luxuries and comforts in our life, but when we start to base our state of happiness on them, we begin to create unhealthy habits. Often, we are so focused on what we don't have that we simply neglect all that has been blessed upon us. The homes we live in, the meals we eat, the access to unlimited clean water, the clothes on our back, the electricity and heat that are so vital and important for us—we forget to appreciate and give thanks. These are the things we need to survive, and Western society labels them "basic necessities," yet there are millions of people across the world who don't have any of them.

How ironic is it that those who are financially blessed often find themselves with daily stress and moments of tension, whereas those living with practically nothing in third-world countries are living carefree and jumping for joy when they finally get access to an ounce of clean water?

Perception is key, and we begin to lose that when we don't appreciate all that has been granted to us. In my own journey through mental health, I began to switch my paradigm of thinking around all that was initially causing me suffering and distress. Although my job was not fulfilling, or what I truly wanted to do, it was still giving me an income. I was grateful to be earning a salary when so many others were searching for employment. I decided to grow with this mindset of appreciation and further give thanks by journaling. I started to research the effects of writing, and it was apparent that it helped in relieving stress, organizing thoughts and allowing creativity to shine . . . and here I am, writing my first book!

It's not always easy, as we are creatures of habit. I spent years feeding the negative thoughts and believing that I was not good enough, but that's when we must dive deeper into ourselves. Consistency is what builds habits, and if we can construct a series of negative behaviours, it's also possible to rewire them into positive stepping stones that can help us evolve into our true potential. When we shift our mindset towards appreciation, we are less likely to attract stress, anxiety, doubts and fear. It reminds us that the road we are on is a series of ups and downs filled with adversity and triumphs. The journey is where your character is built and developed. Thoughts, actions and emotions are unraveled, and healthy habits are brought to life with consistency through discovery and inner work.

DIVING INWARDS

As I've made clear from the beginning of this book (and I will repeat this again and again like a mantra), you are *not* a failure! Repeat after me: "I am *not* a failure!"

As I spent most of my young adulthood living in this notion of fear, uncertainty and anxiety, it became apparent that somewhere along the line I began to pour more fertilizer into this negative mindset, allowing toxic seeds to grow. When I started to work at shifting my thoughts and emotions, the act of appreciating all that I was blessed with began to ripen into encouraging practices. Incorporating the act of gratitude is like receiving the keys to a vehicle and accepting accountability and ownership, and the ability to act is like having a GPS guide you through the roadmap in your journey of life.

It's important to understand that inner work is not all peaches and cream. It can seem like a lonely and depressing task. As a society, we are so conditioned to find external outlets to keep us occupied that many times we believe that engaging in social gatherings and activities is therapeutic. Now, don't get me wrong, sometimes the best thing we can do to unwind is unplug our phones, meet with friends, watch a movie, grab a coffee, go to a restaurant or spend the afternoon getting a manicure/pedicure. It becomes harmful, though, when we don't take the time to figure out why we are experiencing these downfall moments. Without this awareness, we fail to understand that these are patterns that are recycled over and over, only to re-emerge in our lives through different scenarios and situations.

When we really begin to focus on the idea of inner work, it is crucial to apply accountability. This is why I've mentioned it earlier that it's one of the pillars that are needed to guide us through our journeys. Accountability can lead to suffering. This may distress many people, but that is exactly what we must endure to see ourselves to the other shore surrounded by peace and fulfillment. It's quite simple: if you're not willing to accept the errors and mistakes you make, how do you expect yourself to grow, evolve and mature? Growth can be painful, but it does lead to triumph and victory.

The practice is not to cripple your mindset and beat yourself to the ground when acknowledging your faults and virtues, because that won't allow you to get yourself back up and improve. The goal is to be critical and assess why you have chosen to lead yourself towards the path that has negatively impacted your mental, physical or emotional state of being. As you begin to use curiosity to understand yourself in a deeper way, you'll shy away from personal judgement. When we are able to peel away the layers of our reasoning, choices and decisions, oftentimes the root cause of our unhappiness will surface. That's when the magic really begins, because we are now able to construct the habits needed to improve our well-being.

The inner work becomes challenging when we are faced with an unknown outcome. It's not pleasant when we find ourselves digging through old memories of pain, shedding tears and experiencing feelings of fatigue. For many people, the battle within is like stepping into a whole new world. Society for the most part has not been supportive of speaking openly and truthfully about mental health and our overall well-being. This is important to understand because it has caused a major gap between acceptance and general health.

Think about the following example. It's completely okay to stress ourselves and pull an all-nighter when studying for an exam that is worth half of our final grade, yet it's deemed demoralizing to spend a few sessions with a therapist trying to figure out why we are going through stress and anxiety so we can improve our health for the long haul. We can't allow society and external conditions to normalize the current state of mental health. The more we can focus within and create healthy habits, the more accommodating society will be towards the process of self-care. Inner work is getting to know yourself from the core.

Whether you are searching through the realm of spirituality or any other types of inner work, the concept revolves around placing the attention within. This process is difficult for many, due to the way we have conditioned ourselves to think and operate. We don't realize the time and effort we spend focusing on the lives of other people. This has resulted in programming our subconscious minds to continue directing our energy externally to meaningless measures. As you can probably understand by now, the more we pay attention to matters that are not relevant to our well-being, the harder it becomes to improve ourselves from the mind, body and spirit level.

When I began to work on self-discovery and my own healing, it became shocking to uncover how much pain I was unnecessary causing myself for so many years. The beliefs, thoughts and feelings I held within from an early age were beginning to wreak havoc on my health. I was always someone who questioned my accomplishments. I didn't believe in myself and therefore I believed that the voices of others were truthful and reflected reality. My self-criticism and self-doubt manifested into physical sensations. I found myself always catching a common cold or having aches and pain. This was frustrating and embarrassing, to say the least, because I was always someone who preached about fitness and nutrition, and yet here I was feeling unwell most of the time. I believed that nothing good could ever occur in my life and that I would always be someone who barely made it by. This resulted in a mindset of blaming others, being angry within and not accepting the fact that I have the power to rearrange my thoughts. It was evident that my ego and beliefs

were punishing my body the entire
time. This wasn't pleasing to accept,
but it was a relief to finally understand
that I can be in charge of how I react
and choose to be. I made the decision
to accept accountability, and although
the process wasn't pretty, it was needed
if I wanted to experience happiness. I
spent time journaling the thoughts and
habits I had that weren't contributing to
my growth, and the emotions that came
along with them. This was extremely
important, as it helped me shift into
a new routine that would allow me
to evolve as an individual. Now that
I knew what I had planted inside of

my soul for so long, the path towards constructing habits based on a positive mindset became clearer.

Regardless of the circumstance you find yourself in at the moment, you are not stuck. The most disappointing act in thought is believing that your potential is limited and that where you are right now is the only place you'll ever be. That is incorrect. The reason you may feel unworthy, trapped and isolated is because your mindset is clouded by doubts, fears, opinions and beliefs you have conditioned yourself to believe for many years. To move past these hurdles, you must continue to train yourself into a positive state of being. This is where an activity such as reading affirmations can become an asset in your self-care toolkit. Affirmations have proven to help people overcome self-sabotaging behaviours and negative judgements. They can be an important tool to utilize because they rewire the mind to believe in worthiness, success and happiness. There is no right or wrong when it comes to this activity. The goal is to find what works best for you and your authenticity.

Inner work is not just about pausing and reflecting, it's also about indicating what's meaningful to you and taking small steps to build consistency around that. Figure out what excites you and gives you a sense of meaning and purpose. Begin to devote time to that each day, even if it's only for ten minutes. You will be surprised to realize how satisfied you become by simply dedicating time to your interests. While working a full-time job that I was clearly not passionate about, I could sense that my energy was depleted by the end of each day. However, when I began to write and share meaningful content through social media, it began to uplift my spirit. The more awareness around mental health I spread and the more comfortable I become opening myself up to the topic of well-being, the clearer it became that I was meant for this. Inner work has become the measuring stick to align myself towards my purpose, and I believe with all my heart that this applies to every person, regardless of their situation or circumstance.

It is important to realize that every second of every moment of every day is connected to what you need to improve, work on or focus your energy toward. The sooner we are able to apply this understanding, the better it will be for our overall well-being.

CHANGE IN PERSPECTIVE

I've shared a glimpse of my journey, which has been surrounded by setbacks, defeats, triumphs and victories. There is nothing I have experienced that is exclusive to my path. We have all gone through ups and downs and experienced periods of tears and joyfulness. The objective in writing this book is to emphasize hope, achievement, success, contentment and self-belief. So often our mindsets are processed with the wrong nutrients when we find ourselves in difficult situations. Feelings of regret, anger, sadness and trauma emerge when something hasn't gone our way according to what we planned. One of the key elements I discovered when moments of adversity erupted in my life was learning to shift the paradigm. Perspective is such a healthy and important component of a healthy mindset. I want to make this point clear:

building a sense of perspective does not necessarily mean you are running away from reality. The truth is, reality is a mindset. Perspective is being able to look at situations from a different lens that allows us to understand the lesson in a more profound way.

I used to feel pity for myself. I felt I didn't deserve to be treated the way I was or feel the way I felt. Rejection became normal for me in all important areas of my life. I found myself trapped in a job that I despised because of how it affected my physical and mental well-being, and I couldn't walk away because I didn't believe I was good enough to succeed in anything else. I felt my voice was not being heard and I was barely getting by in anything that looked beneficial or promising. I recall moments of walking into the gym feeling upset and ashamed of who I was. Unlike others who can use that as fuel to build themselves physically, I would walk out within minutes of entering just to head back home into my bedroom where I felt secure. What angered me the most was the support I would receive from family and friends. None of their kind and uplifting words made sense to me. All it did was force my rage inside, because I was feeling the opposite way.

When I began to incorporate accountability and take ownership, I noticed a change in how I was operating daily. Instead of listening to music while going for a morning run or doing physical activities, I would find myself immersed in motivational podcasts that helped me look at my situation in a constructive way. I was beginning to pay a lot more attention to developing small yet impactful habits. These small shifts in practices were allowing me to deal with my circumstances in a healthier manner and see things differently for once. I started to understand that there were many lessons I was being taught to receive the strength and courage I always prayed for and needed. God was working for me the entire time, and yet there I was, blinded by attachment and ego. I was starting to realize that most of the stress I was developing was stemming from the notion of control I perceived I had over life. Without letting go and surrendering to reality, I was growing seeds of pain and suffering. All the struggles I had faced were strategically placed on my journey for a reason, just like they are for yours. I needed to cleanse my mindset, which had been tempered with negativity, to build a stronger, more positive and healthier foundation. I began to analyze every situation to find a deeper cause or meaning. Reframing my thoughts helped me tremendously. I didn't view my job the way I once did. Every morning I would start the day with gratitude that I was blessed enough to be given the chance to learn and receive a paycheque. When things got difficult, I would find more reasons to be grateful. In each of the failures and disappointments we encounter lies a lesson that is there to shape our strength and character.

The goal is to create a fabric of joy that allows you to seek growth instead of fuelling your ego. When you begin to apply perspective to the challenges you face, you will often notice a sense of humility. That's where we begin to feel aligned to who we really are. It's also very important to create a sense of pride and accomplishment towards the efforts you are showcasing, instead of feeling resentment towards the circumstances in which you find yourself. This technique has helped me stay in alignment when I've experienced moments of distress. Speaking to yourself in a positive way and diving deep into the reminders of all you have accomplished and done is a game-changer.

This is a difficult task to embark on, and rightfully so. Society tends to put labels on everything to justify its importance. If you're trying to build a business, then having a social media account with fewer than a particular number of followers automatically labels you a failure. If you're not earning a specific amount of income, or if you aren't married and having children by a certain age, society will cast you into feelings of shame and disappointment.

One of the greatest lessons I learned, and continue to be reminded of, is the art of filling your own cup with love and light. Nobody walking on this earth will have the capability of lifting you to your potential. There are always positive influences, examples, stories and people that can spark the change within you, but until you learn to turn on the tap yourself, the water you drink will always leave you dehydrated in life and happiness.

Learn to celebrate the progress you are forming and build from that wave of momentum. Think about this: you may be going through a tough period in your life. Perhaps your career isn't where you envisioned it would be, or you've lost a job, or maybe a relationship has ended and left you feeling broken and in despair. The fact that you are waking up each day and moving forward is an act of power. Believe it or not, there are many people out there who choose not to make the effort or demonstrate gratitude, even when things are going in their favour. That is power for you and a reason to celebrate the milestones you are building. Perspective is fundamental in improving mental health, and the more we are able to reframe challenges and setbacks as opportunities to learn and develop, the less likely we are to indulge in self-sabotaging behaviours.

The keys to the world have always been inside of you, regardless of the situation you find yourself in, and that is your ultimate superpower.

BUILDING YOUR AUTHENTICITY

The concept of authenticity is vital and holds a major link to mental health. Many times, we find ourselves more concerned about our status than our well-being. This behaviour has resulted in many people living their lives in an artificial way, being influenced by those around them. It has become an important area of discussion because of the severely negative effects it has on so many people. The goals, passions, interests and dreams we hold so dearly as children often fade away once we turn into adults. As we get older, there tends to be more periods of stress, fear, want and unhappiness. Without diving deeper into this topic, many people will usually claim that this is just a result of having responsibilities and a mere part of life. Although that may hold some truth on the outer surface, how many of those are truly pursuing their passion and dreams?

Without recognizing the deeper understanding, we've allowed ourselves to be categorized and placed in specific bubbles that disallow growth. Several years ago, when I was applying to jobs in the financial sector, I spent a few days finessing my résumé and cover letter so I would stand out as a potential candidate. During that time, I was extremely proud of my recent accomplishment of gaining a certificate as a health and life coach. My passion was always physical and mental well-being and this was a personal milestone. However, I spoke with a career advisor about improving my résumé, and they suggested I remove that accomplishment. At the time, I understood the reasoning. The financial sector is a different world than nutrition and overall wellness; therefore, I should only have included experiences that were tailored to the jobs for which I was applying. It wasn't until years later that I began understanding mental health in a more profound way. This made me realize that when we work hard to satisfy and please others, we tend to lose ourselves in the process. This became apparent for me because, for close to five years, I held back from pursuing my dream as a health and life coach. The persistence, hard work and the love I carried for being a wellness coach was put away on a shelf out of fear of failure. On a psychological level, my self-esteem and confidence were hindered because of this, and it ultimately had a negative impact on my overall mental health and well-being.

Instead of showcasing what we pride ourselves in through our wants and interests, we run away from our authenticity and begin to wear a badge of false identity. A résumé is a perfect example of this. We spend hours and hours trying to articulate a well thought out piece of paper that indicates why we should be selected for a specific position. In the process, many of us embellish our skills and qualifications hoping to get hired. Many people may not find a fault in this method, as it does not necessarily cause damage to one's self-development, but at what level are you willing to jeopardize your identity?

Looking back, it was the learning and understanding I gained through my health and life coaching program that allowed me to progress and sustain myself in a field that is opposite to it. The program instilled in me attention to detail, patience, persistence and gratitude, and I was able to apply these skills to my daily tasks in the financial sector. When you're speaking to over a hundred clients a day and following a metric system while trying to meet sales quotas, the overload of work can deplete your energy. I was able to channel the teachings of wellness and incorporate several tips and best practices, from breathing exercises to eating specific foods and supplements that allowed me to maintain a positive mindset.

Humans are built to expand ourselves and our awareness. It's understandable that a lot of people are working jobs that don't fulfill their purpose because they accommodate their personal situations or finances. However, we should never stop following those hobbies and interests that give us a feeling of bliss. When you tap into your true inner self, there a force is revealed that aligns you to your purpose. That alone will manifest in many opportunities, but to get there you must continue planting the seeds of self-love while being unapologetically you to the core.

The journey you are on is uniquely designed for you. We must not allow the voices of others to dictate the turns and stops we make on our roadmap. Having authenticity and following your dreams is not a walk in the park, it's quite the opposite. Social media can do a great job of romanticizing the definition of authenticity, but the truth is it's a difficult task. When you decide to listen to the voice within you and pursue what sparks your soul, you are automatically separated from most people. Unlike them, you are not driving on a road that's already been paved by others towards your journey, you're creating your own. When you draw your own roadmap, you will come across potholes, roadblocks and detours that will attempt to stop you from reaching your destiny. The key, however, is to understand that these setbacks are not there to signal failure. They are there to remind you that from difficult lessons will emerge the strength and courage that is required to gain all that you are working for. That is why the journey itself will always hold more value than the destination.

THE TIME FOR ACTION IS NOW

The ability to control your own narrative is powerful, and by doing so you will eventually begin to see doors of opportunities opening in front of your eyes. To get to that awareness, you must begin to prioritize yourself. It's common that, without much thought, we can spend too much time arranging ourselves to meet external needs. The energy, time and money we spend on cleaning up before attending a special event or function, whether it means getting a haircut, doing our makeup or buying a new suit or dress, seems like an ordinary and unproblematic task. When we begin to spend that same energy, resources and time to improve ourselves within, the feelings change. There is often a sense of egotism and selfishness when we place ourselves first. This is why it becomes difficult to say no without being judged as a self-centred individual.

Like many people, I spent a great deal of time trying to please others. I was ignoring the state of my mental health for years until it began to show up negatively through physical and emotional ways. I would find myself catching the common cold often, not being able to eat specific foods due to digestive issues and feeling drained and unhappy. This cycle of continuous torture was repeating itself even when I kept reminding myself that I was going to change and make things better.

When I had hit the lowest point in my life, I made a promise to say no to this form of pain. It wasn't an easy formula to recovery, but I soon felt a feeling of empowerment. Refusing what no longer served me allowed me to take back the energy I gave out to others while setting healthier boundaries. Maintaining the feeling of empowerment soon led to the formation of positive attributes such as confidence, control, clarity and a sense of self-respect, the last one being something I had neglected for a long time.

I never understood the importance of taking back control while prioritizing my own needs and feelings. It became evident that when we really want to say no but continue to fulfill those self-imposed obligations to please others, we begin to create a negative feeling that brings out resentment and frustration. This wreaks havoc on our own lives, and we tend to spread that to others through self-destructive behaviours.

It is not an easy task to reframe negativity into a moment of learning and development. Our conscious mind makes up less than ten percent of our brain, which means the rest of learning and development occurs in our subconscious. The learning behaviours, experiences, habits and basic life functioning we engage in tend to feel auto-piloted, because these habits are stored in the subconscious.

The problem, however, is with the unpleasant experiences we encounter in our lives. We tend to form negative and unhelpful attitudes around these events if we don't choose to address them. This can prevent us from achieving the dreams and goals we desire. Unresolved trauma can be exposed in several ways, including resentment, anxiety, fear and self-doubt. Trauma can also manifest in physiological ways that can keep us from performing to our potential. This is why patience is such a virtue. When we are working towards improving our mindset, we must learn to understand that there are years of built-in programming that have designed the framework of how we think, act and feel. Permanent changes do not develop overnight. Having control of the conscious mindset does require more energy, but it results in greater control of healthier habits, which allows us to achieve our goals and feel content. It's no surprise that the concept of growth and authenticity is so important when working on personal development. It's essential to have goals because they give us a reason to wake up every morning, but the impact of growth holds a far deeper measurement. Unlike goals, there is no real stopping point on the map of life when it comes to your personal growth.

It takes bravery, effort and courage to practice new skills and habits while diving deep within the soul and examining our beliefs. This forces us to disable the act of judgement and perceive with a curiosity mindset. By enacting this thought process, we can become gentler with ourselves, thus creating a progressive outcome. Goals can be linear depending on your behaviours, but when you are able to focus on growing as an individual, you're able to stretch outside of your comfort zone, which allows you to achieve greater results. This process will allow you to become the person you were destined to be: your authentic self.

LEARNING TO SURRENDER

Most of my young adulthood was spent searching for belonging. Being an introvert, I spent my time looking for connection with something. Whether it was a relationship, an idea for a career change or a specific purpose, nothing was satisfying my soul and giving me the sense of fulfillment I was searching for.

Looking back, all the rejections and setbacks paired with the confusion I felt was my intuition forcing me not to settle. We often build a sense of importance around external factors because we neglect a portion of ourselves within. Let me be a bit more specific.

A few years ago, I had applied for a coaching position within the company I worked for. My goal was always to help others and give back, and I felt this opportunity would fulfill my wishes. I was fortunate enough to have an interview with the recruiter. I was extremely nervous going in, but I spoke from my heart and felt that I was going to be hired for this job. I checked off all the boxes that were required and my confidence was beginning to emerge. A week later, however, I was advised that they had gone in a different direction and I was not the successful candidate. I was devastated. Within minutes of hearing this, my digestive system began to crumble, my anxiety amplified and I started to feel depressed and frustrated.

These sensations were nothing new to me. As time went on, I continued to dig deep within and understand myself from the core. I soon began to realize that these moments of failure were not resulting in my deprived state of well-being. It was the meaning I was giving to these situations that were controlling the narrative and my emotions. The job I had high hopes for was put on a pedestal because I felt if I could get the title of "coach," perhaps I would feel confident enough to finally put myself out there as someone who is reputable enough to help others. I was craving a relationship because I felt it would complete a part of me that was empty due to the inexperience and unwillingness of incorporating self-love. I walked around in all directions, not because I was confused, but due to my self-doubt and fear.

Many times there are disappointments that come from being rejected because we feel that those external factors will provide us with a sense of being or belonging. It's completely understandable to feel emotions of sadness, grief and anger over situations that don't work in our favour, but the takeaway is to find the meaning we are giving to these matters. Trusting the process and learning to let go of situations is extremely beneficial to our well-being, but we can't adapt into this mindset without focusing within ourselves by planting seeds of faith, love and kindness.

When you begin to let go, you'll notice a sense of appreciation developing. A lot of the self-sabotaging behaviours and patterns will soon become apparent and unravel effortlessly in front of you.

When I began to let go of what I had no control over, I started to recognize the negative traits within me that were appearing without me recognizing them. During moments of stress and frustration, for example, I would blame factors like the weather for contributing to my unpleasant mood. This would enable more negative behaviours, which resulted in a cycle of self-sabotage. When I began to appreciate more, along with trusting the process, I noticed myself feeling less anxious. If the weather showed periods of rain, instead of complaining that I wasn't able to go for a run outside, I found myself reframing the situation. I would give gratitude that the birds were able to have water to replenish themselves and that the plants were able to grow and absorb nutrients through the soil.

There is so much power brought on by letting go. Not only do you find yourself more liberated and connected to self-love, you also begin to see the importance of prioritizing your own well-being. You'll begin to understand that the external factors so many people are mired in are merely a substance of temporary convenience. The importance of spiritual growth, inner peace and maturity will always outweigh the status of one's salary, the gadgets and vehicles they own and their looks. There are many people that are extremely wealthy but living unhappy lives. There are many people that are complimented on looking beautiful from the outside but are involved in toxic and negative behaviours. Until we stop searching within ourselves and focusing on self-care, the only seeds that will be harvested will be those of low-grade qualities.

Life experience is the most valuable apprenticeship you can receive. The setbacks, the failures, the adversities, the obstacles and the downfalls are all lessons that are given to us throughout our lives, it is how we choose to grow from them that will shape our character.

So many of us are searching for a sign, and it's simple: You are *here*. That is your gift and blessing, and that's all you need to know. Continue to focus on inner growth. Cultivate habits of kindness and compassion. Keep believing in yourself regardless of the odds stacked against you. It's moments like these in which strength and courage build. Dream on. Carry on. Show up. Rise up.

Printed in Great Britain
by Amazon

85330866R00059